SWEDEN
the people

April Fast and Keltie Thomas

A Bobbie Kalman Book

The Lands, Peoples, and Cultures Series

Crabtree Publishing Company

www.crabtreebooks.com

The Lands, Peoples, and Cultures Series

Created by Bobbie Kalman

Coordinating editor
Ellen Rodger

Project editor
Sean Charlebois

Production coordinator
Rosie Gowsell

Project development, design, editing, and photo research
First Folio Resource Group, Inc.
  Erinn Banting
  Molly Bennett
  Tom Dart
  Alana Lai
  Jaimie Nathan
  Debbie Smith
  Anikó Szocs

Prepress and printing
Worzalla Publishing Company

Consultants
Marita Karlish, Archivist/Librarian,
American Swedish Institute

Photographs
AFP/Corbis/Magmaphoto.com: title page, p. 26 (left), p. 27 (bottom);
Ragnar Andersson: p. 5 (bottom); Bettman/Corbis/ Magmaphoto.com:
p. 6 (right); Jonathan Blair/Corbis/Magmaphoto.com: p. 22 (top), p. 30
(top); Jan Butchofsky-Houser/Houserstock: p. 24 (left); S. Carmona/
Corbis/magmaphoto.com: p. 24 (right); Corbis/Magmaphoto.com: p.
11 (left); Lars Dahlström/Tiofoto: p. 17 (right); Francis J. Dean/
Corbis/Sygma/Magmaphoto.com: p. 16; Macduff Everton/Corbis/
Magmaphoto.com: p. 13 (left), p. 18 (left), p. 20 (bottom), p. 25 (top);
Ales Fevzer/Corbis/Magmaphoto.com: p. 5 (top); Giraudon/Art
Resource, NY: p. 8 (top); Hal Horwitz/Corbis/Magmaphoto.com: p. 3;
Dave G. Houser/Houserstock: p. 14 (left); Hulton Archive/Getty
Images: p. 6 (left), p. 7; Len Kaufman: p. 4 (bottom); Layne Kennedy/
Corbis/Magmaphoto.com: p. 27 (top); Bosse Kinnås/Tiofoto: p. 18
(right); Erich Lessing/Art Resource, NY: p. 9 (right); Buddy Mays/
Corbis/Magmaphoto.com: p. 15 (bottom); Nationalmuseum,
Stockholm, Sweden/Bridgeman Art Library: p. 9 (left); Richard T.
Nowitz: p. 29 (bottom); Richard T. Nowitz/Corbis/Magmaphoto.com:
p. 21 (right); Lena Paterson/Tiofoto: p. 23 (bottom); Steve Raymer/
Corbis/Magmaphoto.com: p. 15 (top); Réunion des Musées
Nationaux/Art Resource, NY: p. 10 (right); Raymond Reuter/Corbis
Sygma/Magmaphoto.com: p. 14 (right); Reuters NewMedia
Inc./Corbis/ Magmaphoto.com: p. 25 (bottom), p. 26 (right); Jan Rietz/
Tiofoto: p. 4 (top); Ted Spiegel/Corbis/Magmaphoto.com: cover;
Stapleton Collection/Bridgeman Art Library: p. 8 (bottom); Stapleton
Collection/Corbis/Magmaphoto.com: p. 10 (left);Hans Strand/
Corbis/Magmaphoto.com: p. 17 (left), p. 31; Trip/Ask Images: p. 29
(top); Trip/M. Feeney: p. 20 (top); Trip/Tom Paley: p. 30 (bottom);
Trip/Steve Ross: p. 24 (right); Tomas Utsi: p. 12, p. 13 (right), p. 19,
p. 28 (left); Dan Vander Zwalm/Corbis Sygma/Magmaphoto.com:
p. 11 (right), p. 28 (right); Bo Zaunders/Corbis/Magmaphoto.com:
p. 21 (left), p. 22 (bottom), p. 23 (top)

Every effort has been made to obtain the appropriate credit and full
copyright clearance for all images in this book. Any oversights, despite
Crabtree's greatest precautions, will be corrected in future editions.

Illustrations
Dianne Eastman: icon
David Wysotski, Allure Illustrations: back cover

Cover: A Swedish girl prepares for a day of cross-country skiing.
Sweden's forests, beaches, and mountains make it an ideal place for
outdoor sports and activities.

Icon: A *stuga*, or cottage, appears at the head of each section. *Stugas*,
found throughout Sweden's countryside, are usually painted red
and white.

Title page: A mother and grandmother blow bubbles at a *midsommar*,
celebration in Stockholm, in the east. *Midsommar* celebrates the arrival
of summer.

Back cover: Herring, silvery fish that grow to be 10 inches
(25 centimeters) long, swim in large schools in the Baltic Sea, off the
eastern coast of Sweden.

Note: When using foreign terms, the author has followed the Swedish
style of only capitalizing people and place names.

Published by
Crabtree Publishing Company

PMB 16A,	612 Welland Avenue	73 Lime Walk
350 Fifth Avenue	St. Catharines	Headington
Suite 3308	Ontario, Canada	Oxford OX3 7AD
New York	L2M 5V6	United Kingdom
N.Y. 10118		

Thomas, Keltie, 1966-
  Sweden, the people / Keltie Thomas.
    p. cm. -- (Lands, peoples, and cultures series)
"A Bobbie Kalman Book."
Includes index.
**Summary: Explores how the history, climate, and geography
of Sweden have shaped the customs and practices of its
people, looking at daily life in both the city and the country.**
  ISBN 0-7787-9328-1 (rlb.) -- ISBN 0-7787-9696-5 (pbk)
  1. Sweden--Social life and customs--Juvenile literature. [1.
Sweden--Social life and customs.] I. Title. II. Series.
DL631.T523 2004
948.5--dc22
                                        2003016180
                                        LC

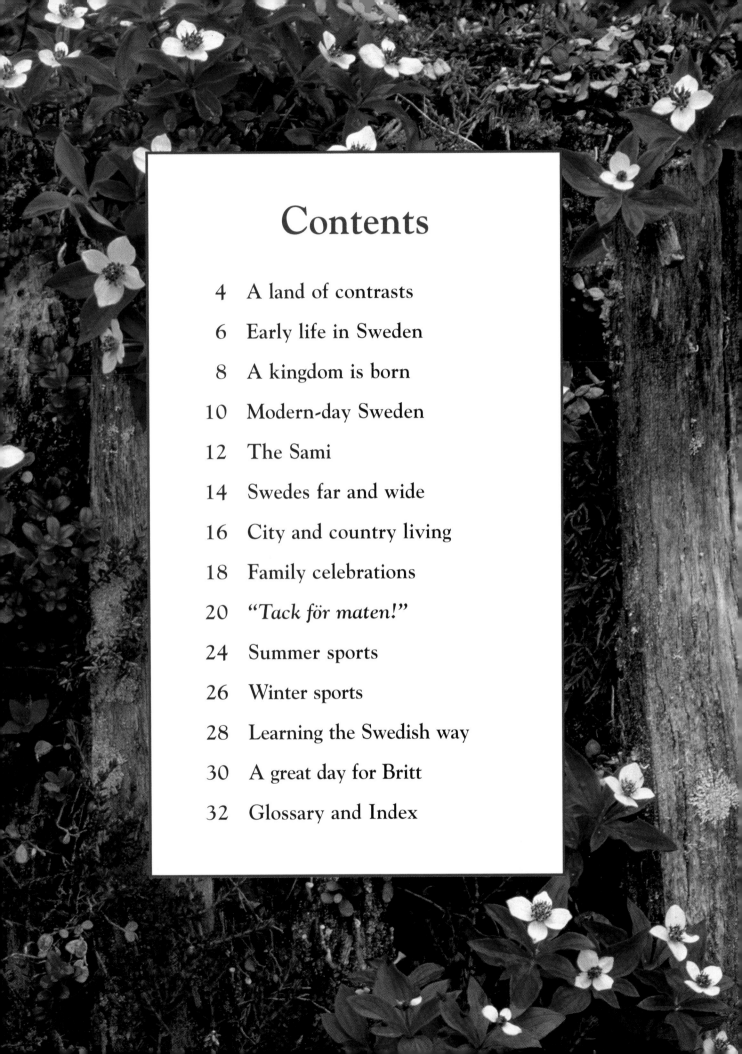

Contents

A land of contrasts

Not far from the **North Pole** is the country of Sweden. It shares a stretch of land called the Scandinavian Peninsula with Norway, to the west. Mountains and deep lakes cover the northern and western parts of the country, while forests, beaches, and rocky coasts fill the south.

In the north and south

Life in northern Sweden is very different from life in the south. Winters in the north last seven to eight months, and there are weeks when the sun barely rises. No matter what time of day people go to work in the mining, **logging**, or tourism industries, they travel in the dark. When summer finally comes, there are weeks when the sun never sets. Many homes have thick, black blinds on the windows to block out the light

A Sami man prepares to ride a sled pulled by a reindeer. The Sami, believed to be Sweden's first inhabitants, use reindeer for milk, meat, hides, and transportation.

Swedes stroll through a street in Gamla Stan, the oldest part of Sweden's capital, Stockholm.

Tennis fans, with faces painted to look like the Swedish flag, cheer at a match in Stockholm. Tennis is the most popular sport in Sweden.

Going to work

Most Swedes live in the warmer south. They work in factories that manufacture computers, telephones, and medical equipment, in stores, banks, schools, and in tourist areas. Many also work for the government, developing educational, employment, and healthcare programs that give Swedes one of the highest **standards of living** in the world.

Having fun

When they are not at work, Swedes hike in the country's mountains, swim and boat in the many lakes, and cross-country ski during the snowy winters. People also get together with family and friends for special celebrations, such as birthdays and weddings, where they sing, dance, and share a traditional *smörgåsbord*, or buffet, with dishes such as salmon, pickled herring, and smoked reindeer.

Children in traditional clothes play before their cousin's wedding outside Malmö, a city in the south.

Rock paintings of hunters carrying axes and spears have been found on large boulders in Tanum, in the west. Scientists believe the paintings were done by the Sami more than 3,000 years ago.

Around 10,000 years ago, when a very cold period in history known as the Ice Age ended, the Sami people arrived in Sweden and in the areas now known as Norway, Finland, and Denmark. They grew crops, gathered berries and roots, hunted and herded reindeer, and caught herring off the northeastern coast.

The Sveas and Goths

The Sveas and Goths arrived in Sweden from present-day Germany sometime before 100 A.D. in search of land. The Sami moved north, while the Sveas settled in the central region of Sweden, now called Svealand, and the Goths settled in the southern area, now called Götaland. The Sveas and Goths farmed, raised cattle, fished, and traded with countries in central Europe. They exchanged furs, **bronze** tools, and silver coins for wine, silk, and spices.

Land of the Sveas

The Sveas and Goths were divided into kingdoms that frequently fought for control of the country. By 500 A.D., the Sveas dominated the central, eastern, and southern parts of present-day Sweden. The region came to be known as *Sverige*, or Sweden, which means "Land of the Sveas." They also fought for control of neighboring lands, including what is now Norway, Finland, and Denmark. Kingdoms were ruled by chiefs, who protected the people that worked on their farms and sailed their ships along trade routes.

The Vikings

Sweden prospered, but by 800 A.D. the country faced extreme overpopulation. Most Sami had been pushed to the far north where the land was more difficult to farm. Chiefs from Sweden and other countries in northern Europe, such as Denmark and Norway, left to conquer land and establish trade routes. These chiefs came to be known as Vikings, which means "pirates," because they were fierce warriors who often robbed the people they conquered.

Viking longships could be used to sail in the rough ocean or sneak up on enemies on narrow rivers.

The Swedish Vikings

The Swedish Vikings set out to present-day Russia and the Ukraine, to the east, and as far south as present-day Turkey. In each place they raided, they set up trading posts. Control of trading posts made Sweden one of the richest nations in the world.

Viking government

The Vikings were feared for their violent raids, but at home they followed an orderly system of government. Viking communities were led by *jarls*, or earls, who were wealthy landowners. *Jarls* employed *karls*, people who worked as farmers, **merchants**, fishers, or craftspeople. Individual communities were organized into provinces headed by chiefs and kings who made laws. Each community and province had a court called a *thing*. Members of the *thing*, who were elected by the communities, appointed chiefs and kings, settled disputes, and made sure laws were followed. This system of government, based on elections, is the model for democratic governments around the world today.

The end of the Viking era

Vikings worshiped gods and goddesses who they believed controlled nature. In the early 800s, **missionaries** from Germany began to introduce Christianity to Sweden. Christians believe in one God and in the teachings of his son, Jesus Christ. Around 990, Olaf Skötkonung, who ruled a province in the southwest, declared himself king of Sweden. He **converted** to Christianity, and made it Sweden's official religion.

People who agreed to adopt Christianity were given money and the land of those who refused to convert. **Rebellions** broke out and those who fought to keep their beliefs were beaten and even killed. Vikings were divided and their kingdoms and trade routes were taken over by King Skötkonung's supporters. This strengthened the power of King Skötkonung's government and put an end to the Viking era in Sweden.

In this illustration, Vikings fight English sailors attacking their trading post.

Sweden was united by the mid-1100s, but two wealthy families, the Sverkers, who dominated the province of Svealand, and the Eriks, who dominated the province of Götaland, fought for control of the **monarchy**. The monarchy changed hands between the Sverkers and Eriks many times over the next century.

When Erik Eriksson, the last king of the Eriks line, died in 1250, his nephew Valdemar Birgersson was made king. Valdemar Birgersson was only seven years old at the time, so his father, a *jarl* named Birger Jarl, ruled in his place. During the time he ruled with his son, Birger Jarl strengthened the central government, built royal palaces, and encouraged German merchants to settle in Sweden. Swedish towns, such as Stockholm, grew into powerful cities and centers for trade.

Magnus Ladulås

King Valdemar ruled from the time of his father's death in 1266 until 1275, when he was overthrown by his brother, Magnus Ladulås. Magnus Ladulås eliminated all traces of the Viking system of *jarls*, and instead created a noble class. Nobles were members of wealthy families given land by the king in exchange for fighting against his enemies. Peasants farmed the nobles' land.

The Kalmar Union

At first, the king and nobles were very powerful, but over the next hundred years, merchants gained control. Many nobles blamed the loss of land and power on the poor leadership of their king, Albrekt of Meklenburg. They turned to Queen Margareta I, ruler of Denmark and Norway, for help. Queen Margareta I had been married to a **descendant** of Magnus Ladulås. In 1389, the army of Queen Margareta I defeated King Albrekt, and she united Sweden, Finland, Denmark, Norway, and Iceland into a single kingdom called the Kalmar Union.

Magnus II Eriksson, the great-nephew of Magnus Ladulås, ruled Sweden between 1319 and 1363. During his rule, he also controlled Norway and conquered Finland.

Queen Margareta I died on a ship sailing to Norway in 1412 while she was still queen of Sweden.

The Stockholm Bloodbath

The Kalmar Union lasted more than a hundred years, but many Swedish nobles were unhappy because they believed that nobles from Denmark and Norway were given more land and more power in the government than they were. Swedes rebelled against Denmark and fought to regain control of their country. In 1520, King Christian II of Denmark decided to put an end to the rebellions. He invited a group of Swedish nobles, politicians, and **nationalists** to a banquet. When they sat down to eat, he ordered that the heads of more than 80 of the men, viewed as rebels, be chopped off. The event came to be known as the Stockholm Bloodbath.

Vasa's rule

One rebel, Gustav Vasa, had escaped from a Danish prison in 1519. He returned to Sweden the next year. When he heard about the bloody banquet, he rallied troops to rebel against the Danes. The Swedes won the rebellion, the Kalmar Union was dissolved, and in 1523, Vasa was elected king.

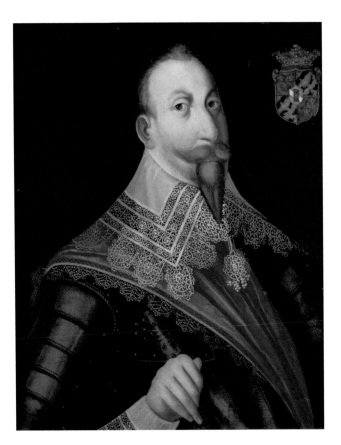

Gustav II Adolphus ruled Sweden from 1611 until his death in 1632. He was killed in battle during The Thirty Years' War.

At war

From the mid 1500s to the early 1600s, Sweden fought with Russia, Poland, and Denmark for control of trade in the Baltic Sea, to the east. Grain, iron, copper, lumber, and furs passed through the Baltic region for trade in other countries. By 1611, Sweden had gained control of the main Baltic sea ports. During the Thirty Years' War, fought among several European countries between 1618 and 1648, Sweden also gained control of northern Germany and parts of Denmark and Norway.

The end of the power period

The Great Northern War, which began in 1700, ended Sweden's era as a superpower in Europe. During the war, Denmark, Poland, and Russia joined forces to fight Sweden for the land they had lost. By war's end in 1721, Sweden was stripped of all its territory except Finland, which it had controlled since 1335.

Gustav Vasa gathers troops in Dalarna, a region in central Sweden, to help him fight the Danish in 1520.

Modern-day Sweden

From 1718 to 1772, Sweden went through a period known as the Age of Freedom. Power shifted from the monarchy to the Riksdag, or Swedish Parliament. Sweden experienced struggles for power among political parties, wars, and a famine, or severe shortage of food, during this period, but it was also a prosperous time for trade, industry, art, and culture.

The Napoleonic Wars

In the 1800s, most countries in Europe were involved in the Napoleonic Wars. The wars were led by Napoleon Bonaparte, emperor, or ruler, of France, who wanted control of Europe. King Gustav IV Adolph, the last descendant of Gustav Vasa, led Sweden into battle against France in 1805. Sweden defeated France, but wars with France's **allies**, Russia and Denmark, followed in 1807 and 1808. Sweden could not defend Finland, and had trouble defending itself against Russia. Unhappy with the leadership of King Gustav IV Adolph, a group of government officials rebelled and removed him from the throne.

Sweden's monarchs are still descendants of Jean-Baptiste Bernadotte, the French general who became king of Sweden.

Jean-Baptiste Bernadotte

Peace with Russia was finally established in 1809, and Sweden gave up its control of Finland. The loss of the territory divided Swedes about who should rule their country. They decided they wanted a strong leader who could make Sweden powerful again, so in 1810 members of the Riksdag offered the throne to a general in Napoleon's army, Jean-Baptiste Bernadotte. Bernadotte changed his name to King Carl XIV Johan and joined countries, such as Russia and England, that had turned against Napoleon. By the end of the wars in 1813, France lost much of its territory. For its participation in the war, Sweden was given control of Norway.

Swedish troops prepare for battle against the French during the Napoleonic Wars.

The Industrial Revolution

The **Industrial Revolution** swept over Sweden in the 1800s. New machinery made it faster and easier to farm, to extract **natural resources,** and to produce large quantities of goods such as steel, explosives, and paper products. Fewer people were needed to work on farms, so they moved to cities in search of jobs. The population in cities grew so much that many people could not find work and lived in extreme poverty. Between 1850 and 1930, nearly 1.5 million people left Sweden for other countries in Europe and for North America in search of a better life.

After **World War II**, Sweden's economy shifted again when demand for cars, **telecommunications** equipment, medicine, and other products manufactured in Sweden increased. Sweden quickly became one of the wealthiest countries in the world.

In this illustration from the 1800s, groups of Swedish immigrants arrive in the United States in search of jobs and a better life.

The Swedish royal family participates in official ceremonies and celebrations, but has no real power in the country.

Sweden today

Sweden has been a welfare state since 1932, which means that the government pays for many job, housing, medical, and educational programs with money it raises through high taxes. Laws are made by the elected Riksdag, which is headed by the prime minister. Sweden still has a monarchy, but many Swedes believe it should be dissolved because the king only plays a symbolic role. In 1809, Sweden became the first country to have an ombud, who protects people against injustices that government officials commit. Today, many countries have ombuds of their own to protect the rights of their citizens.

Choosing peace

Sweden has not gone to war since 1814. When the country's new constitution was written in the early 1800s, it included a policy of neutrality, which means that Sweden would not get involved in conflicts between other countries. Sweden followed this policy during World War I (1914–1918) and World War II (1939–1945), and still does today. In 1995, when Sweden joined the European Union, a group of countries that promote trade among themselves and other countries, it joined under the condition it could remain neutral in any war.

According to a legend told by the Sami, the Sami god Ibmel had two sons. They lived in Sweden's far north before the last Ice Age covered the land in snow and ice. When the snow began to fall, one brother escaped to the south and hid in a cave. The other brother braved the storm in the north. The Sami believe they are descended from the brother who braved the cold.

Most of the nearly 20,000 Sami who live in Sweden today survive by hunting, fishing, and herding reindeer in the far north, as their **ancestors** did. Industrialization and the promise of better jobs in cities have caused many Sami to abandon their traditional lifestyles. To protect the culture and rights of their people, the Sami created an independent parliament that works with the Riksdag.

Nothing wasted

The Sami use the reindeer they herd for meat, milk, and hides. Reindeer meat, which is rich in vitamins, is cooked or dried. Reindeer milk is used to flavor coffee and is made into cheese. Warm clothes and boots are made from reindeer hides. The Sami use other parts of the reindeer too. In fact, *aello*, the Sami word for reindeer herd, means "what one lives on." Reindeer tongue and marrow, from bones, are considered delicacies. *Lappkok*, a broth made from boiling reindeer marrowbones and liver, is a favorite Sami meal. Reindeer blood is used in pancakes and sausages.

(top) A Sami father and son mark a reindeer calf to show that it belongs to their herd.

Life of a herder

Sami communities, called *siida*, center around the reindeer herd. People in each *siida* follow their herd as they migrate to mountain grazing pastures in the summer and to forest grazing lands in the winter. Many Sami now have two homes — one near the summer grazing lands and one near the winter grazing lands.

The tradition of reindeer herding in Sweden is threatened because homes and mines are being built where reindeer once grazed. A Sami committee works with the Riksdag, making claims on behalf of Sami forced from their land. If the Sami can show that a *siida* has used the land for more than 90 years and that herds depend on it, the government allows the Sami to continue using the land.

A Sami woman wears traditional clothing decorated with red, yellow, and blue embroidery.

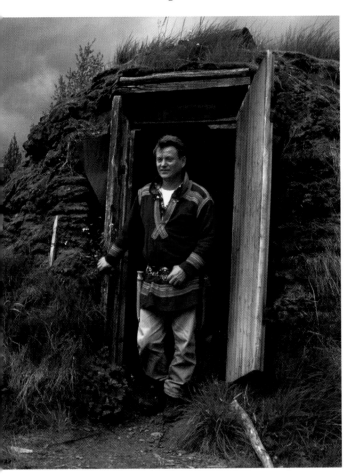

A Sami herder comes out of his summer home. Many Sami dwellings are made from materials such as wood, stones, and mud that are found near the grazing lands.

A distinct language

The Sami speak a language related to Finnish called Sami. The dialect, or version, most widely spoken in Sweden is Central Sami. Central Sami has many words for the same thing. For example, *sahpah* and *saevrie* both mean "snow," but *sahpah* is light snow and *saevrie* is thick snow. At first, the Sami passed down their language orally from generation to generation, but some words and stories were lost. Now, it is a written language that is taught in Sami schools. There are also Sami TV and radio shows, and books and magazines are published in Sami.

Religious beliefs

Today, most Sami are Christian but many also hold the traditional beliefs of their ancestors. The Sami believe there are spirits in nature. Gods and goddesses, such as Bieggaålmaj, the god of wind, control nature. To keep the gods and goddesses happy and to ensure the Sami have success in herding, farming, and health, the Sami hold ceremonies in which they give gifts, or offerings, to the gods and goddesses. The offerings are usually reindeer blood or fat, which the Sami consider valuable.

Swedes far and wide

The Finnish

Along Sweden's border with Finland are several Finnish communities. Immigrants from Finland arrived in Sweden in three waves: first in the 1500s because of wars in their country; next after World War II; and finally in the 1960s in search of jobs in manufacturing. Although the communities follow many Swedish traditions, they still speak the Finnish language at home, in schools, and in church. People also sing traditional Finnish songs accompanied by a *kantele*, a stringed instrument that is Finland's national instrument.

A woman dressed in a traditional Swedish vest, scarf, hat, and skirt welcomes visitors to the Skansen Open-Air Museum in Stockholm. The museum has a collection of houses and buildings that show how people lived and worked in Sweden hundreds of years ago.

Most Swedes are descended from the Sveas and Goths. Others are descendants of Vikings from Sweden, Denmark, and Norway. They still celebrate their **heritage** and practice the traditions of their ancestors. People tell stories recorded in *eddas*, which are long poems about Viking gods, goddesses, and heroes. Many of the stories are about Thor, the god of thunder, who had a magic hammer that shot out flashes of lightning. Craftspeople carve statues of Thor out of stone or wood, and make necklaces and bracelets decorated with charms shaped like Thor's hammer. They believe the charms will bring them luck.

Thousands of Swedes gather in Stockholm to celebrate the birthday of the country's king.

Coming to Sweden

Since the end of World War II, other immigrants have arrived in Sweden in search of jobs and to escape poor living conditions and wars in their **homelands**. In the 1960s, along with the Finnish, immigrants arrived from Russia, Yugoslavia, Turkey, Greece, West Germany, the United Kingdom, Poland, and Italy to work in the manufacturing industry. Recently, **refugees** from war-torn Bosnia-Herzegovina, Iran, and Iraq have settled in Sweden. The Swedish government promotes **multiculturalism** and encourages immigrants to practice their own religion.

The people of the Åland Islands

Åland is an archipelago, or group of islands, in the Baltic Sea. The islands are part of Finland, but were owned by Sweden until 1809. Their more than 25,000 inhabitants are of Swedish ancestry. They speak Swedish, follow Swedish traditions, and consider themselves Swedish citizens.

Children at a daycare center ride tricycles while waiting for their parents to pick them up. The Swedish government funds many childcare programs to help parents who work.

Cyclists take a break on a rocky coast near the city of Mariehamm, on the Åland Islands.

Cities in the south are home to 85 percent of Sweden's population. The rest of the population lives in towns and villages in the southern, central, and northern parts of Sweden.

Life in a city

Many Swedish cities, such as Stockholm, in the east, Göteborg, in the west, and Malmö, in the south, grew out of Viking trading settlements. They became centers for the manufacturing of steel and ships in the 1800s. Today, people in cities still work in manufacturing industries — especially in factories that produce cars, telecommunications equipment, and medicine. They also work in the tourist, medical, and service industries.

City homes

Most Swedish city dwellers live in houses and apartment buildings, many of which were built by the Swedish government to ensure that people had comfortable, affordable housing. Most houses and apartment buildings have playgrounds, parks, and gardens nearby where people relax and play. Among modern homes and apartment buildings stand palaces, factories, and government buildings that are hundreds of years old.

Friends chat at a busy café, people shop, and tourists take in the sights in downtown Malmö.

Stugas, or cottages, line the bay in Trgsunda, a fishing village in northern Sweden. Some people live in the red and white cottages year-round, and others rent them out in the summer to people from the city.

Life in the countryside

Nestled among forests and lakes in central Sweden are small villages and towns where people live in *stugas*, or cottages. *Stugas* are made of wood and are usually painted red with white trim around the doors and windows. People also live on farms scattered between villages. The farther north a person travels, the fewer villages there are. Some villages are so remote that shops not only sell groceries and household supplies, but they often double as a gas station, post office, or bank.

Going on vacation

Some farmhouses have been renovated and turned into vacation homes for people who live in the city. Many Swedish businesses shut down for the entire month of July so people can take a vacation. People also vacation on Sweden's coasts, on its islands, and in its national parks. Some families stay in the city during their vacations to visit museums and art galleries, to watch concerts and plays, and to take part in festivals such as *midsommar*, or Midsummer, which marks the beginning of summer.

Country celebrations

Country festivals draw thousands of people from all over Sweden in summer and winter. Jokkmokk, one of Sweden's northernmost towns, has held the annual Winter Market for nearly 400 years. Sami craftspeople, dressed in traditional clothes made from reindeer furs and colorful, embroidered fabric, sell baskets woven from roots, finely made leather clothes, and knives with carved handles of reindeer bone. The Sami perform *joiks*, or funny songs made up on the spot, while spectators watch people race reindeer on a frozen lake.

A girl rides a reindeer sled. In very remote parts of the far north, people use reindeer to get from place to place because there are very few roads.

Baptisms and confirmations

Not long after they are born, most babies are baptized in the Church of Sweden. Parents and family watch as a minister gently pours water over the baby's forehead to officially welcome him or her to the Church. When children are thirteen, they are confirmed, or made full members of the Church. To prepare for the ceremony, the children attend confirmation camps, which are special classes that teach them more about their religion.

A family enjoys a birthday picnic in the countryside, where the girls collected wildflowers for their mother's present.

Swedes celebrating a birthday are awakened to a greeting of "*Grattis på födelsedagen!*" which means "Congratulations on your birthday!" Families bring the birthday person a breakfast tray with coffee, a sweet roll, and a candle.

At a *kalas*, or birthday party, friends and family eat cake, open presents, and play games. Adults have birthday open houses on their "even" birthdays, which are every ten years. People come throughout the day to drop off cards and gifts, have a snack, and wish the birthday person a long and happy life.

A baby is baptized, or made a member of the Church of Sweden. The Church of Sweden has been Lutheran, a denomination of Christianity, since Gustav Vasa ruled between 1523 and 1560.

Getting married

Whether Swedes get married in a church or at a park, they follow traditions to bring them luck. At one time, bridesmaids carried bouquets of herbs to keep evil spirits away during the ceremony. Today, it is traditional for the father of the bride to put a silver coin in his daughter's left shoe. The mother of the bride puts a gold coin in her daughter's right shoe.

The bridal crown

During the ceremony, many brides wear silver or gold crowns set with precious stones, crowns made from **myrtle** leaves and flowers, or headbands wrapped with colorful ribbons that hang down their backs. These resemble the silver crowns decorated with flowers that Viking brides wore. After the ceremony is a dinner and dance. When the wedding reception ends, the newly married couple leaves for a trip called a *smekmånad*, which means "first month of marriage." A *smekmånad* is like a honeymoon that lasts a month.

Sami family traditions

Long ago, Sami families gathered in villages to celebrate spring's arrival before they set off to their summer grazing grounds. Many people got married during these celebrations, and still do today. Brides and grooms sometimes dress in traditional red and blue embroidered clothes. Brides also wear veils topped with a wreath of flowers. During the wedding ceremony, the bride is given a ring identical to the one the groom gave her when they were engaged. When the couple has a baby boy, the husband gives the wife another identical ring.

A couple is married at the Ice Hotel in Jokkomokk, in the far north. The Sami rebuild the hotel, which is made entirely of snow and ice, each winter because it melts each spring.

"Tack för maten!"

Whether they are finishing breakfast, lunch, or dinner, Swedes say, *"Tack för maten!"* which means "Thank you for the food!" On special occasions, a short toast is given at the beginning of dinner. People raise their glasses and say, *"Skål,"* which is like "Cheers," but means "drinking vessel." *Skål* comes from the Viking word for "skull." According to legend, Vikings used the skulls of their enemies as cups.

Mealtime

Most people in Sweden eat a breakfast of toast; *messmör,* a soft, sweet cheese; hot or cold cereal with *filmjölk,* a fermented milk that tastes like yogurt; and juice or coffee. In the past, Swedes sat down to their largest meal of the day, *middag,* at four o'clock in the afternoon. Many people in the countryside still follow this custom, but most city dwellers have a lighter lunch around noon and eat their main meal in the evening. For lunch, Swedes enjoy *smörgås,* or sandwiches made with one slice of bread heaped with a combination of meat, fish, cheese, and vegetables. At dinner, people serve meat or fish and potatoes along with cheese or fruit.

Traditional meals

One traditional Swedish meal, served mainly in the north, is *surströmming,* which means "rotten herring," although the fish is not rotten at all. Before there were refrigerators, people used to preserve fish by salting it, but salt was very expensive, so they only used a little. As a result, the fish had a very strong smell, which is how it got its name. Another popular dish is *gravad lax,* or marinated salmon, which is made by rubbing salmon with salt, sugar, and herbs. *Pytt i panna,* a hash made from meat, onions, potatoes, eggs, and pickled red beets, is a tasty dinner dish.

During midsommar *celebrations in June, people eat traditional dishes such as* inlagd sill, *or pickled herring, with sour cream, chives, and new potatoes.*

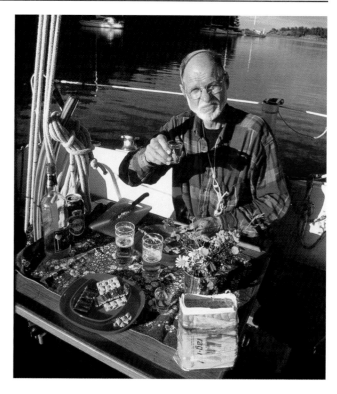

Swedes often toast with snaps, *an alcoholic beverage made from potatoes or barley. The drink is flavored with caraway seeds and spices such as cumin and dill.*

Knåckebröd

Knåckebröd, or crispbread, is a traditional Swedish bread made of wholemeal rye. It was first made in central Sweden, where there was only enough water to run flour-grinding mills in the spring and fall. Since the flour would not keep for six months, people used it to make a thin, hard, cracker-like bread. Enough *knåckebröd* was made to last from one milling season to the next. The bread, which had a hole in the middle, was stored by hanging it on a pole above people's wood stoves.

Crabs, caught mainly on the western coast, are in season in the summer. People steam them or use their meat to make pasta sauces or crab cakes.

Seasonal ingredients

Some ingredients are only available at certain times of the year. In the summer, people pick and buy sour berries called lingonberries. They use lingonberries to make fresh jam that they spread on everything from pancakes to meatballs. In August, families and friends celebrate the end of summer with a feast of crawfish, which look like small lobsters. The crawfish, which they often catch themselves, are boiled over an open fire, seasoned with dill, and served with bread and spiced cheese. Summer's end is also the season for wild mushrooms. Mushrooms that are safe to eat, such as cepes, chanterelles, and ringed boletuese, grow in dark, mossy parts of Sweden's forests. They are used to make sauces, soups, and salads.

A waitress carries a basket of crunchy knåckebröd. *Spices added to* knåckebröd *give it different flavors.*

Take your pick

In the 1500s, people put out bread, meat, and cheese for *smörgås* that people could snack on before they sat down to their main meal. This tradition evolved into the *smörgåsbord*, or "open sandwich table," which is a banquet-like feast that consists of five separate courses. Pickled, salted, and marinated herring make up the first course. Salmon, other fish, smoked reindeer, and roasted mutton leg follow in the second course. Cold cuts make up the third course. Hot dishes, such as Swedish meatballs and Jansson's Temptation, which is a casserole of baked potatoes and anchovies, make up the fourth course. The fifth and final course is made up of desserts, such as fresh fruit, ginger snaps, and rice pudding.

Swedish meatballs are different from the meatballs eaten in North America. North American meatballs are usually served with tomato sauce and pasta, while Swedish meatballs are served with a cream sauce or gravy.

Meals for special occasions

On special occasions, fancy dishes are added to the *smörgåsbord*. At Christmas, for example, Swedes serve *lutfisk*, which is dried salted codfish soaked in lime, sausages made from beef or pork, mustard-glazed baked ham, and sweet and sour red cabbage. They also serve "Dip in the Pot," a broth in which people dip bread.

At Christmas, Swedish families prepare smörgåsbords with special dishes for people to sample.

Tjock pannkaka

Tjock pannkaka, or Swedish egg pancakes, are served for breakfast or as part of a *smörgåsbord*. Swedes top them with lingonberry jam, but any jam or applesauce can be used. You can make these tasty Swedish treats with the help of an adult. This recipe serves six people.

You will need:
4 eggs
1 1/2 cups (375 ml) flour
1 teaspoon (5 ml) salt
1 1/2 cups (375 ml) milk
1/4 cup (60 ml) butter
jam, jelly, or applesauce

What to do:
1. Beat eggs. Add flour and salt.
2. Stir in milk.
3. Melt butter over stove in a cake pan.
4. Pour batter in the pan and bake pancake at 400° Fahrenheit (200° Celsius) for 30 minutes.
5. Remove and let stand for a few minutes.
6. Cut the pancake into six pieces.
7. Serve with jam, jelly, or applesauce.

The Sami have eaten reindeer meat for centuries, but recently the meat has become popular in other parts of Sweden and around the world. Reindeer meat is stewed, grilled, broiled, and roasted. It tastes like beef, but is lower in fat and higher in vitamins.

A mother and daughter enjoy ice cream cones for dessert.

Tennis

Björn Borg, Stefan Edberg, and Mats Wilander made tennis Sweden's most popular sport. In 1976, when Björn Borg won his first of five straight Wimbledon championships, a tennis tournament played every June and July in England, children and adults grabbed rackets and headed to tennis courts. Many Swedes learn to play tennis from a very early age and thousands compete in the Donald Duck Cup, the country's largest junior tennis tournament.

The annual marathon in Stockholm winds through the capital city's streets, parks, and along its many waterways.

Canoeists, sailors, hikers, picnickers, and campers visit Sweden's national parks during the warm summers. Swedes also play summer sports such as golf, tennis, and soccer, or run in races, such as the 19-mile (30-kilometer) *Lidingöloppet*. Between 25,000 and 30,000 people from more than 25 countries run this cross-country race, which is held on Lidingö, an island northeast of Stockholm. There is also a shorter version of the race for children called the *Lilla Lidingöloppet,* or "Little Race."

Tennis player Björn Borg won eleven major tennis championships before retiring in 1983 at the age of 26.

A couple cycles through Borensberg, a town in the southwest.

Allemansrätten

Swedes have a tradition called *allemansrätten*, or "everyman's right." Everyone has the right to hike, picnic, camp, ski, cycle, swim, and boat anywhere they want — even on private land. They are also allowed to pick mushrooms, berries, and wildflowers, except those protected by law. People take the privilege very seriously, and are careful not to damage the natural environment or people's properties.

Gymnastics

The handsprings, cartwheels, somersaults, and flips performed by gymnasts around the world were invented by Swede Per Henrik Ling. In the early 1800s, Ling opened the Royal Gymnastic Central Institute in Stockholm, where he developed the exercises and taught teachers how to train people to strengthen their bodies and make them more flexible. Today, children and adults take gymnastics lessons, and Sweden has a national team that competes in the Olympic Games.

In 2002, Annika Sorenstam broke the Ladies' Professional Golf Association (LPGA) record for winning the most events in one year.

Winter's ice and snow bring people out to ski down mountains, snowshoe across the cold landscape, and skate on frozen lakes and canals, or manmade rivers. Cross-country skiing is one of Sweden's most popular winter sports. In March, thousands of Swedes strap on their cross-country skis and participate in the 53-mile- (86-kilometer-) long Vasaloppet, or "Vasa Race." The race celebrates Gustav Vasa's trek across Sweden in 1523 as he gathered troops to join him in the fight for Swedish independence.

An American goalkeeper blocks a shot by Swedish player Jorgen Jonsson during a world championship hockey game.

Ice hockey

Indoor hockey rinks are open all year, but in the winter, people use frozen lakes and rivers to practice their game. In Sweden, people play a different version of hockey than that played in North America. Players skate on a larger ice rink and there is no center line, which allows them to pass the puck further. Many of Sweden's best hockey players, such as Mats Sundin, Nicklas Lidstrom, and Markus Naslund, play on both the Swedish national team and in the National Hockey League (NHL).

The winner of the Vasaloppet, the longest cross-country skiing race in the world, crosses the finish line.

Bandy

Bandy is a fast-paced game that is a cross between ice and field hockey. It is played on ice rinks the size of soccer fields by teams of eleven players. Bandy uses a ball instead of a puck, so the players have to skate very quickly to keep up. In Sweden, Norway, Finland, and Denmark, there are professional bandy leagues and competitions.

Dogsledding

In the north, dogsledders, called "mushers," race teams of dogs over ice and snow for hundreds or even thousands of miles. Siberian Huskies and Alaskan Malamutes are the best sled dogs because they are strong and fast. Each dog wears a harness that is attached to a gangline, which the musher holds as he stands on a sled and yells commands that mean "speed up" or "turn right." Sweden has a national dogsledding team that competes in races around the world.

Bandy balls are made from cork, a type of tree bark, and are covered with hard rubber, which makes them durable.

In many parts of Sweden, such as Jokkmokk, people hold races in which reindeer pull racers across snow and ice on sleds.

Learning the Swedish way

Grundskola students take a break from their reading to make a collage.

Once children in Sweden turn six or seven, they go to *grundskola*, or compulsory school. Swedish law requires all children to attend *grundskola* for nine years. Most children go on to *gymnasieskola*, or upper secondary school, for three years after that. The Swedish government pays for books, supplies, transportation, and even lunch.

Grundskola

Children learn reading, writing, math, science, history, music, physical education, religion, woodworking, and sewing in *grundskola*. In the third grade, they also study English, and in the sixth grade, they choose another language to learn, such as Sami, French, German, or Spanish. Students in Sami towns in the far north study the same subjects as children in other Swedish schools, but they learn them in Sami.

No report cards

Unlike in North America, Swedish children have the same teacher from grades one to three and grades four to six. The teachers do not give report cards or marks until the eighth grade. Instead, parents come to meetings two or three times a year to talk to the teacher about how their children are doing in school.

Gymnasieskola

From grades nine to eleven, children who attend *gymnasieskola* take courses that prepare them for university or the workplace. Students begin to explore jobs that interest them and go to work in hospitals, schools, mechanical shops, or factories for up to fifteen weeks of the school year. They choose from seventeen programs of study, including industry and crafts; agriculture and forestry; technology; language and social services; economics and office work; or caring professions, such as healthcare and nursing.

Students in gymnasieskola discuss Swedish literature, one of their main subjects. Other main subjects include English, mathematics, and science. Sami is taught in areas with high Sami populations, and courses on Sami literature, religion, and culture are offered in universities throughout the country.

After graduating from Uppsala University, north of Stockholm, students are greeted by family and friends carrying flowers and signs with pictures of the students when they were young.

Students learn how Swedish people lived hundreds of years ago during a field trip to the Nordic Museum in Stockholm.

A great day for Britt

Britt is excited to show her cousin Inge what life is like in Stockholm.

Britt woke up, yawned, then rolled over to go back to sleep. When she remembered that it was Saturday, she jumped out of bed. Britt and her cousin Inge had been e-mailing back and forth all week, counting down the days until Inge and her parents arrived in Stockholm. Inge's family lived on a farm near Rajsjö, north of Stockholm.

Britt had so many fun activities planned. They would skate on the canal, have a *smörgåsbord* with Inge's favorite foods, and maybe even build a snow fort with the other children in the community playground.

Britt ran downstairs and found a steaming hot bowl of cereal and *filmjölk* waiting for her on the table. She ate as quickly as she could.

"Not so fast, Britt," her father said. "You'll make yourself sick and you won't be able to skate." She and her father laughed.

Just then, there was a knock on the door. Britt jumped up from the table and answered it. When she saw Inge, she gave her a big hug. "I'm so glad you're finally here," she exclaimed.

While Britt's and Inge's parents ate breakfast, Brit showed Inge her bedroom. Inge admired the ribbon that Britt won in the sixth grade science fair.

Inge and her family live on a farm where they raise cattle.

"I did a project on different kinds of mushrooms," Britt explained.

"I love picking mushrooms," Inge added. "Near the farm are lots of forests where mushrooms grow. You should come visit this summer."

"I would love to!" Britt agreed.

After breakfast, everyone bundled up in hats, parkas, and snowpants, and headed to Tunnelbanan, the subway that took them to the canal.

Inge had never been to Stockholm before and was surprised when she saw that all the islands were connected by bridges and canals. "It's like that city in Italy," Inge exclaimed. "That is why people call it 'Venice of the north,'" Inge's mother explained.

When they arrived at their skating spot, Britt and Inge laced up their skates as fast as they could, fastened their helmets, and they were off. They raced to see who could cross the canal first. When they got tired, they sat by the canal's edge and shared a snack of *knäckebröd* and cheese.

After a few hours of skating, they decided to go to Gamla Stan, or Old Town, at the center of Stockholm. To get there, they took a ferry. Inge thought it was fun to travel around the city by boat.

"Some of the buildings in Gamla Stan were built by the Vikings," Britt said.

"I'd like to live there!" Inge said as she pointed to Kungliga Slottet, the palace where the royal family lives.

After a long day of skating and sightseeing, it was time to go home for a *smörgåsbord*. They got back on Tunnelbanan and headed for home.

Britt's mother covered a long kitchen table with all kinds of food. Inge was excited. She loved reindeer meat and Swedish meatballs. There was also herring, cheese, bread, and her favorite, Jansson's Temptation. To top it all off, they had cake, pie, and pudding. Britt and Inge ate until they were stuffed. After supper, everyone had coffee and Britt's uncle played songs on the fiddle while the families sang along. It was a great ending to a perfect day.

(top) The sun begins to set over Stockholm as early as one o'clock in the afternoon during the winter.

Glossary

ally A country that helps another country, especially during a war

ancestor A person from whom one is descended

bronze A metal made by melting copper and tin together

convert To change one's religion, faith, or beliefs

descendant A person who can trace his or her family roots to a certain family or group

heritage Customs, objects, and achievements handed down from earlier generations

homeland A country that is identified with a particular people or ethnic group

Industrial Revolution A shift from an agricultural society to a society that produced goods in factories

logging The cutting down of trees in a forest

merchant A person who buys and sells goods

missionary A person who travels to another country to spread a particular religion

monarchy A government that is ruled by a king, queen, emperor, or empress

multiculturalism The existence of various cultures within a society

myrtle A tree with sweet-smelling white flowers and shiny leaves

nationalist A person who wants his or her country to be independent

natural resource A material found in nature, such as oil, coal, minerals, or timber

North Pole The most northern point at which Earth tilts on its axis

rebellion An uprising against a government or set of rulers

refugee A person who leaves his or her home or country because of danger

standard of living The level of comfort and wealth of a society

telecommunication The science and technology of sending electronic messages by telephone, computer, radio, or television

World War II A war fought by countries around the world from 1939 to 1945

Index